Too Young To Worry

Joan E. Bishop

Pen Press Publishers
London

© Joan E. Bishop 1999

First published in Great Britain by
Pen Press Publishers Ltd
39-41 North Road
Islington
London
N7 9DP

ISBN 1 900796 02 3

A catalogue record for this book is available
from the British Library

Original illustrations by Mr. Luckhurst,
brother-in-law to the author

Front cover design by Catrina Sherlock

Dedication

I wish to dedicate this book to the memory of my dear mother the late Mrs Edith Rosa Bishop. Through her undaunting efforts she tried to ensure that we lived as normal a life as possible during a terrible war. I also wish to include all mothers in a similar position to us and the women who looked after other people's children during the long war years 1939 - 1945.

Foreword

This book is about my eventful childhood memories and impressions of World War II. I have tried to incorporate my fears and feelings at the time and also to include some of the major historic events of the war, and how these events affected my dear sister Eileen and myself.

Although sixty years have passed the memories will be with me for the rest of my life. Some are very sad and others amusing.

This story is completely true and all details given of the War events are correct as far as I know.

CONTENTS

Chapter One

My Home in the Country
(*Evacuation experiences*)

In the August of 1939 I was nine years old and a very happy child, living with my dear sister Eileen aged eleven at the time and my very attractive and kind mother who was thirty-nine. My father was serving with the Royal Navy on HMS Aurora. He had spent many of my childhood years abroad serving with the Navy in China and various places all over the world.

During the August of 1939, my cousin Pamela aged eleven was spending her school summer holidays with us. We lived in Elson which was a very new estate not completely finished. We had previously lived in the upstairs large flat over a shop in High Street, Gosport and when we moved to Elson (a district of Gosport) we considered that we lived in the country. During this last peace-time school holiday my mother took us out a lot and a favourite outing was to the large shopping centre at Commercial Road, Portsmouth and we enjoyed the short ferry boat crossing Portsmouth Harbour (England's premier Naval Base). Crossing the harbour on a peacetime sunny August afternoon one could see Admiral Nelson's flagship, HMS Victory, (in dry dock in Portsmouth Harbour). A short trip from the 'Hard' - after watching the mudlarks at play in the muddy shores of Portsmouth Harbour - we arrived at the busy shopping centre - unaware that it was to be obliterated by German Bombs in the coming year! We enjoyed visiting the open air swimming pool in Gosport and enjoyed splashing around in the icy cold water with many other kids. My sister, Eileen, had a new bicycle during these, (for us) carefree days. I remember the song South of the Border was popular at that time.

Mum had bought Eileen a brand new navy blue school uniform which Eileen was itching to wear, as she was to commence studying at a new school 'The Central School' at the beginning of the September term. At this time all children attending Secondary Schools were obliged to wear the school uniform and Eileen's consisted of a white panama hat with a red and navy striped school band - a navy and red tie. At this time I attended Grove Road School, Gosport and girls of my age would normally wear a gymslip with black woollen stockings (except in the summer months).

Towards the end of August when the school holidays were drawing to a close the schools re-opened early and our summer holiday was cut short

At the new school the teaching staff strongly urged the children to tell parents that all

July 1940
Eileen and Joan with their mother,
carrying gasmasks

1939
Eileen and Joan just before the war

CHILDREN SHOULD BE EVACUATED AND THEY WERE MOST EMPHATIC THAT NO CHILDREN SHOULD REMAIN IN GOSPORT. Eileen was informed that younger sisters (or brothers) could accompany the whole school WHICH WAS TO BE EVACUATED to the country - and there were assurances that sisters would not be separated. ALL SCHOOLS IN GOSPORT closed and parents were informed that if they wished to take advantage of the evacuation arrangements, they should take their children to Gosport Railway Station on Friday 1st September 1939 for departure to the country and safety.

Looking back, I realise that my dear mother must have wondered what to do - my father was on the high seas - somewhere! In the circumstances, in view of the advice given by the authorities and the fact that war appeared to be looming blackly on the horizon, she packed our clothes. Eileen wore her new school uniform (in totally different circumstances than envisaged) and of course we had to take our gas masks - they were kept in a cardboard box with string for a handle. These were issued to everyone in England in 1938 when there was a scare of war prior to the Prime Minister Mr. Chamberlain's meeting with Adolf Hitler.

I remember clearly the gathering of the children and teachers at Gosport Station. After our 'goodbyes' to Mum - Eileen and I boarded the steam train which slowly left our dear home town, our dear mother and the life we so loved in peaceful 'old England'. It was such a big adventure for a little girl of nine years old for it was the first time away from home without 'Mum'. I remember travelling through several little stations, one of them was 'Brockhurst'. The building is still there. It was quite exciting travelling on the steam train. My sister looked very smart in her new school uniform and we all carried our gas masks and little bundles of clothes (or cases). After what seemed to me like an endless journey we left the train (I believe at Botley station). At this station we were supplied with some rations and mine included biscuits, chocolate and a tin of corned beef. I was not familiar with the word 'ration' at the time and as a child assumed that this was a false alarm and there would not be a war - just like the scare in September 1938 when trenches were dug in the recreation ground at Elson.

We were taken by bus (I believe) to a village called Hedge End and this was to be our 'safe' retreat. The children walked in a crocodile along the village's country roads in twos, accompanied by a teacher, presumably delivering the children to the very kind people who had promised to accept evacuees.

Looking back, it must have been a mammoth task for the authorities as until that time they had no idea how many children would require homes. In fact, we did not know ourselves that we were to be evacuated until that very morning. One of the teachers took Eileen and I into a very nice bungalow and an elderly lady (she seemed elderly to me) opened the door. She was most upset as she had promised to take in two girls, but due to her husband's ill-health could not take us. This caused a problem for the teacher/organiser. As we walked along the village roads some local children tagged on and appeared very interested in the excitement and all the new children in the village. One girl of eleven told the teacher that if there was no place for Eileen and I she was sure her mother would take us in and on this invitation we went with the girl to her home. What a shock for her poor mother to have two children to live with her - unexpectedly. Presumably some arrangement was made between the teacher and the eleven year old girl's mother.

Eileen and I were 'dumped' way out in the country. The girl's mother was very very kind and appeared to like us immediately, as did all the family. This lady was considerably older than our Mum and apart from the daughter aged eleven had a grown up family - there was another daughter aged fourteen and yet another aged sixteen and also a granddaughter was staying with the family. The bungalow stood in about five acres of ground. There were only two bedrooms and after much family discussion it was decided that Eileen and I would share a bedroom with four others. It was all great fun. In bed I overheard the lady discussing Eileen and I with an older married daughter who had 'fallen in love with us'and wanted us to stay with her. Despite this, the lady of the house wanted us to remain. She also liked us and felt sorry for us having to leave home.

The next day was Saturday 2nd September. We had a good look round the farm and countryside. There were two dogs chained up the whole period of our stay, they were barking all the time. Apparently, there was a 'foot and mouth epidemic' and every time we ventured along the lane from the bungalow we had to dip our feet in a bucket of disinfectant. Our first experience of life in the country - great fun for a nine year old - no main drainage, a well provided our water supply and this was in the yard at the back of the bungalow. They had a couple of horses, and lots of land with a large orchard - and one thing that scared me much more than the thought of war - a big cesspool - I was scared of being pushed into it by one of the local youngsters. Eileen and I got on well with the others and the fourteen year old appeared to be 'in charge' of us. The lady of the house and her husband were market gardeners and went out every day - presumably, to market with one of the horses and cart. Unfortunately the man suffered from fits so the lady had to accompany him. Still we were quite capable of looking after ourselves!

The sixteen year old was very sophisticated in our eyes and was always singing the latest song Mexicali Rose. The family seemed amused and surprised when Eileen and I wanted to have a wash and clean our teeth.

In the orchard there were lots of old bikes some without saddles, wheels, handlebars - but great fun to play with. During this period Eileen and I were trying to adjust to life in the country. We did not like the old toilet outside in the yard and I wondered where or when it would get seen to. All the water had to be taken from the well. Only oil lamps in the evening; everything so different from the modern little house we had left in Gosport.

I remember 'Uncle Mac' speaking to us on the Radio and the song *Goodnight Children Everywhere*, your mother thinks of you tonight and I wondered what Mum was doing in Gosport without us and knew that she would be thinking of us! It was sad I felt like crying.

The following morning Sunday 3rd September we went into the orchard to play with the old bikes and then at 11 am the Prime Minister, Mr. Chamberlain, announced that we were at war with Germany. I am ashamed to say that we all cheered and ran around very happy. It only goes to show that a nine year old had no idea what was in store for the country for the following five years. All I thought about was learning to ride a bicycle! I thought I had my priorities right!

Following the outbreak of war the school authorities arranged for us to visit the village school on a regular basis to check in only to see we were OK. We received no schooling at all. I remember the song Ten Pretty Girls at the Village School and thought it must apply to the village school at Hedge End.

Eileen and I tried to help with the household chores and helped in the grounds picking up potatoes and also picking strawberries from the September crop. My mother had found out where we were and made the tedious journey from Gosport on the bus. She brought some warmer clothing for us and made friends with the family. She could see that they were very kind to us and we had plenty to eat although I believe she thought we were beginning to run wild and looked like gypsy children! On occasions we were taken on the horse and cart to market and we settled down to country life. Towards the end of September it was Eileen's birthday and we missed our life in Gosport and home, but tried to make the best of the circumstances we were in - at the time the song Birthday of the little Princess was popular.

After a month Mum arrived one day and had decided to take us back to Gosport and home to live with her despite what might happen. After our goodbyes to the new family we boarded the bus for Gosport and when we arrived it was dark. I shall never forget the complete darkness of our Avenue not a crack of light anywhere - it was the Blackout - the war had begun. I was surprised, perhaps a little shocked, to find out that during our absence six soldiers who were stationed in a field opposite our house were billeted with us. They slept on the floor in the front (lounge) room which at the time was empty. They were all about twenty-one and were Territorials and guess what? They took it in turns to run beside me whilst I was learning to ride my sister's bicycle! It pleased me and gave them something to do.

Life was so different from the carefree days of August but children soon adjust to life even in a house full of soldiers - but that's another chapter! My cousin Pamela spent the war years in South Africa and we did not see her again until two years after the end of the War.

Chapter Two

Our Soldiers

(The story of six soldiers billeted with us)

On return from evacuation in the country we endeavoured to settle down to life in wartime Gosport.

Our house Aurora was the end house of a block of six and building was completed in October 1937 when we moved in. As war commenced the Estate was incomplete and there were still fields all around us. There was a 'right of way' next to our house which led to the little country Church and across the fields we could see the Guildhall at Portsmouth. In the field opposite our house the Service authorities had stationed six soldiers and they set up their camp in the field. Their Gun Emplacement consisted of sandbags round some 3.7 or 4.5 guns, this made up the Ack Ack site or the correct term being Anti Aircraft Gun Emplacement site. The young men pitched their tents. Comfortable, no I don't think so. As a nine year old I could have told them the field was very damp for I often tramped over it in my wellington boots and sometimes the water ran over the top of the boots wetting my feet.

11

I believe the whole Estate, which was acquired from the Admiralty, had been under water at one time.

The first six soldiers to be stationed in the field were Territorials so I suppose were trained to a degree. Their cooking facilities in the tents were totally inadequate and they were all young men about twenty-one years of age. I think I have already portrayed my mother as being a very kind person, and, in addition she was exceptionally patriotic - as I think most people were - and still are - in a crisis. One day Mum was working on the front garden and one of the soldiers shyly approached her to ask if she could 'pop' a bread pudding in the oven for the lads. Of course, she agreed, and it transpired that they had no idea how to make a bread pudding, so Mum made the pudding for them. It was delicious and these young, hungry, healthy men remembered their own mother's home cooking and felt a little homesick. It became a regular occurrence; mother made puddings and cooked their dinners for them. The Army authorities were very generous with the men's rations - large joints of meat - but no-one stopped to think if the lads could cook, especially with the abysmal cooking facilities, and, let's face it, the soldiers had never left home before. In those days no-one left home until they married and very few people went away on holiday. Holidays abroad were virtually unknown to the poorer and middle classes. The middle classes were not poor - but they were not rich either.

With regard to money, the average wage for a man at this time was about £3 per week. Mum and Dad purchased our house in 1937 for about £700 with the aid of a mortgage (it is now worth about £70,000). At this time Mum and Dad had not been able to furnish our lounge or front room and it was empty except for canvas on the floor and a hand-made woollen rug which Dad had made whilst on board ship. In addition Mum kept her valued upright piano. This room was very convenient for Eileen and I to play in with our many toys. Please don't get the impression that we were poor, as the rest of the house was very nicely furnished and Eileen and I had a very attractive oak bedroom suite with twin beds, and we always had plenty to eat, nice clothes and enjoyable outings to local beauty spots, and I had always assumed we were quite well off! During the period of our evacuation we certainly saw another side of life.

Mum continued with her war effort in helping the soldiers with their food and my Dad was somewhere at sea. One day an Army Officer knocked at our door and asked if he could come to discuss a matter with Mum. He said 'I Understand you have been very kind to my men and I thank you for this. As you are the nearest house to their emplacement gun I would like to billet the boys in your house.' - the six men would sleep in our house each night.

Mum was flabbergasted and said, 'I am sorry, I could not accommodate the men, for one thing I do not have enough bedrooms'. The Army Officer looked around the house and informed Mum that the empty front room would be admirable for the Army's requirements and the men would sleep on the floor in sleeping bags provided from the Army stores. The Officer said it was our duty to billet the men. Mum pondered for a moment and knew in her heart that she would welcome any kindness shown to her husband or brothers who were serving somewhere, and she rather reluctantly agreed that the six young soldiers could be billeted in our house.

The first six Territorials who were billeted with us left the camp and were sent to France and at that time the song *'Somewhere in France'* with you was very popular. Everyone shuddered at the words *'...being sent to France...'* as they knew our boys were probably ill-equipped to deal with the victorious German Army which was sweeping across Europe at an alarming speed.

Six more soldiers were brought to the Army Site and quickly made themselves at home on the site and in 'our home'. Mum laid down some rules for them. For instance, they were required to enter the house by the sideway door so that their muddy boots (or in some cases plimsoles) would not tread all through the house. She moved her piano from the front room to the dining room and the men had the use of the empty front room and the kitchen and outside toilet and garden. Mum always left cocoa, coffee, tea milk and sugar and cakes and biscuits available for them, so that if they came in late they could have a hot drink. She left coal, wood and coke so that they could light a fire.

I am not sure if the second group of men were Territorials or enlisted men, but again, they were all about twenty-one with a Corporal in charge. They came from all walks of life. Some were office clerks and one was a musician (a pianist) I believe for a well-known band it was either Lew Stone or Lew Prague, and often the band played on the radio and he would make us listen and point out the part he played, at the time I thought fancy not playing the whole song. They were very pleasant men and we soon got very fond of them. Sometimes Mum would invite them into 'our room' and the musician would play her piano and everyone would sing. My mother had a lovely singing voice and was popular with them. Looking back, at the time she was a very attractive thirty-nine year old, but was several years older than the soldiers and I think they looked upon her as an 'Older sister', or 'mother' figure. It is sometimes a little inconvenient having six soldiers billeted at the house and every evening they brought their guns and rifles through the house to check the ammunition and sometimes I helped them with this. I am not sure if a couple of the soldiers remained on the site overnight with the heavier guns. One of the men was a little careless and every time he came into our narrow kitchen with a heavy gun or rifle on his shoulder he swung round to speak to us and knocked the wall with his gun. This happened nearly every day and the plaster on the kitchen wall was so badly damaged we could almost see into the next door house!

One of our neighbours had a big Alsatian dog called 'Mick' and this dog was very lively and ran around all over the area, particularly the field where the soldiers were stationed. He quickly made friends with the men and no doubt they gave him scraps of food, and every time one of the men crossed the field to visit his billet 'our home' Mick would accompany him. The soldiers played with the dog and all the children in the neighbourhood used to hang around the site. Practically every empty site in Gosport was used as an 'Ack Ack Site' or Barrage Balloon Site and the young service men and women soon became popular members of the community and attended local socials and dances and the little cinema where the latest films could be seen. At the time a visit to the cinema was a very popular way to spend an evening and sometimes, especially on a Saturday evening long queues would form to see one of the films. The admission price ranged for one shilling (5p) to the really good seats in the circle 3/6 (17½ pence in Decimal money) - very expensive!

On a regular basis the Army Officer would call at the site presumably to pay the men and check that everything was OK. On one occasion Mick the Alsatian was on the site, and when the Officer shouted a command the dog flew at him, and one

'You men keep that Alsation dog in order'.

of the men who was standing at attention had to hold the dog. Needless to say, the Officer was very annoyed but could not do much about it, except suggest that the men should not encourage the animal.

We never knew where my Dad was - 'somewhere at sea' but when the Radio newsreader said 'The Admiralty regrets to announce the loss of His Majesty's Ship...' all our hearts used to stop for a moment for we knew Dad was in great danger defending 'our homeland'. His Cruiser was often referred to as *The Silver Phantom* and earned a reputation for its daring exploits in pursuit of the German Navy whilst avoiding the ever increasing U Boat menace (this was the name given to the German submarines). After the declaration of War we saw nothing of Dad. His manoeuvres took him from Iceland and Spitzbergen in the North to Alexandria, Malta and Gibraltar in the Mediterranean Sea. It was a sad day for this country when the Radio announced the loss on 14th October 1939 of *HMS Royal Oak* at Scapa Flow, with the loss of 810 lives.

Mum wrote every day to my father and her bold handwriting was very distinctive and apparently on board the *Aurora* they always knew when Dad had a letter. Despite all Mum's letters informing him of life in wartime Gosport and our evacuation, and events in our locality, there was one thing she omitted to tell him. He was always at sea and never seemed to come home. She did not want to worry him about us, and for this reason she did not tell him about the six soldiers billeted with us.

As the first Christmas of the war approached we decorated our home and prepared for yet another Christmas without Dad. During all my childhood my father had served in the Royal Navy and spent many years at a time abroad. He spent three years in China on a Gunboat which I believe was called *The Bee* and in the course of his duty sailed almost 2,000 miles up the River Yangtze - his Gunboat went as far as was navigable for its size. This was in the 1930's when Japan attempted the conquest of China and, in addition, there was a little trouble amongst the Chinese who were living under appalling conditions at the time. In addition many years were spent in the Mediterranean areas, Spanish Civil War. It was nothing new for us to have 'no daddy' at Christmas.

On the afternoon of Christmas Day Mum invited the Army boys, who were themselves spending the Christmas away from their loved ones, into our living room to listen to the King's Speech at 3pm in the afternoon on the Radio. I remember his kind voice giving us confidence to face the years ahead. In those days portable and transistor radios were unknown and if one wanted to listen to the 'wireless' as we called it, one sat down in the living room to listen and relax, similar to the way we sit and watch the television or video film today. We all drank the King's health with a small glass of sherry and settled down to make the most of the war Christmas. The King's two daughters, Princess Elizabeth (our present Queen) and Princess Margaret were just young girls like Eileen and I, in fact, we were often called the two little Princesses.

At the time the impact of rationing had not fully been felt as most people had stocked up their cupboards during the 1938 Crisis. As per usual we all retired to our respective bedrooms at a reasonable hour and the six lads slept on the floor of the lounge in their sleeping bags.

During the night the front door opened and in walked a forty year old tall and handsome Naval man. It was my father. He had been given a few hours leave and took the first train from Scotland to Portsmouth. He walked into the lounge. What a shock - there were six men sleeping on the floor!

We were so pleased to see him and he soon accepted the reasons why the boys were billeted with us. In fact, being a Serviceman himself he very quickly got to know them and they all became friends. After Christmas Dad returned to the Aurora and the weather turned exceptionally cold. I remember one day the milk standing on the doorstep froze in the bottle. The bottle did not break but the frozen liquid rose upwards and appeared many inches above the bottle. Mum tried to make us all as comfortable as possible and kept the house nice and warm. The Army fellows were only supposed to remain in the house during the night-time hours and by Service rules were required to stay on their Gun Site. So they spent many hours either in the open or in the little tent. I have already mentioned how damp their field was and in addition everything was frozen to add to their discomfort. We liked all the soldiers but we did have a favourite and his name was George, he always seemed to wear plimsoles, joking, and generally keeping everyone's spirits up. One day, when it was exceptionally cold he called in at the kitchen and fainted in my Mother's arms. As she revived him he confessed that he did not think he could stick the Army much longer, for the conditions were so bad for the men trying to exist in the tent. It was so cold! Mum was horrified to think that her 'boys' should be suffering so and the conditions were so bad. Imagine yourself existing, not for a week, but for the whole winter in a tent - not a luxury one at that. In those days the winters seemed and were so much colder. My mother was old enough to remember horror stories of life in the trenches in France in the 1st World War and was only too aware that the men had to be tough to survive under these dreadful conditions. However, she felt strongly that if the winter continued these men, who after all were only used to office jobs and were not hardened soldiers, would not survive to fight and go to France, and with these views in mind and being a very determined woman she decided to sort the matter out!

In a road called 'Spring Garden Lane' there are some very big houses and one of these houses was requisitioned for the Army Officers. Mum put on her best and smartest hat and coat and plucked up the courage to knock the big old Victorian door. A Junior Officer answered and demanded to know what my mother wanted - mother demanded to see the Commanding Officer and after some hesitance and argument was ushered into a delightful big lounge where several officers were sitting in big easy chairs, drinking and chatting. There was a roaring fire in the big fireplace and the whole atmosphere oozed with luxury not known to most people at the time, and certainly different from the tent in the field. My mother explained how the soldier had fainted and demanded that they provide better facilities on the gun site for the six soldiers. At first the Commanding Officer was very offhand and said the men had to be toughened to the Army Ways but after much argument Mum pointed out that the men would not survive to fight in France if no action was taken and Mum threatened to take the matter to a higher level. At dawn the next day some builders were on the site and erected a fairly large Nissen corrugated iron hut for the men, which although not really comfortable was certainly an improvement on the tents which the men had been forced to survive in.

The six soldiers were very appreciative of the action taken by my mother and between them tried to make that hut as comfortable as possible with pieces of canvas and mats on the floor, and it certainly proved a protection against the icy winds blowing from the harbour over the exposed field. We used to have an old wooden rocking chair which Eileen and I used to play on and Mum let them have this chair and several other pieces of furniture.

All the time the soldiers were with us Mum continued to cook for them and I remember them bringing over really big joints of meat for her to roast. Food was rationed for us civilians and our meat allowance was almost laughable. Remember at the time, we were a big meat eating country, and most people had a joint of meat a couple of times a week during peacetime conditions. The Soldiers were very grateful for our help and unbeknown to me told Mum to take a little of the meat for our consumption sufficient for our needs. I can picture the scene today even after sixty years of mother taking a great huge joint of beef out of the oven and cutting off some scrumptious slices for our dinner from the tasty joint of meat. I was convinced that we would be arrested for taking this meat, but despite this, I ate it not knowing that Mum had been told to help herself!

After a time our six soldiers were posted abroad, presumably, to France, and after a few tears they were collected in a lorry. They bought us some lovely chocolates and Mum tried to comfort them with wise words on a tearful departure by saying 'Remember, whatever happens, pray to the Lord above for strength.' Immediately after these soldiers left another six men came and the routine continued. We soon got to know them and grew

24th October 1939

fond of them and they carried on the tradition of playing with Mick the Alsatian dog. He did so love being with these young men. Mum continued to cook for the soldiers who were shortly to risk everything for their King and country.

During these dark winter evenings Mum, Eileen and I would sit in semi-darkness with the cheerful blaze of a log fire burning and we would talk, sometimes, Mum would read us a story called Coral Island which we liked very much, and we would always have a small glass of Taragona, a sherry type wine, presumably, she thought this would supplement our diet. Regrettably, we hardly ever saw an orange or lemon or grapefruit during the war years and I did not see a banana for the whole of the war.

One evening when chatting, I happened to mention to Mum that I had always wanted a pair of roller skates, that I would like to try skating which was very popular at the time. Along the Avenue the surface of the road was very smooth, hardly any traffic and very suitable for the youngsters to play on and it appeared to be the Headquarters for the skating children of the neighbourhood, many of whom were our friends. Immediately, Mum said 'put on your hat and coat on we will get you some skates' and we went to a well known sports shop in Stoke Road and Mum purchased the skates for Eileen and me. What joy, what fun, every moment of my life was spent on these skates, I pictured myself as a junior Sonja

Henie the famous Ice Skating Star. I learned to skate backwards, could turn quickly and felt I could do anything on wheels - I used to like to show off in front of 'my' soldiers, and anyone else who was interested.

During this time none of the schools were open, so I had plenty of time to skate. Mum tried to keep our education going and Eileen and I would read aloud. She would also give us spelling tests and we tried to keep our arithmetic and mental arithmetic up to standard, we also practised 'our tables' by heart, and I have found this has been invaluable during my life in helping me calculate sums quickly.

After a few months the third group of soldiers received their orders to leave, and this time they were not replaced - they packed up the gun-site, left the Nissen Hut which Mum had fought so hard for and again we said our farewells. There were a few tears for we had become very fond of these young men. They presented Mum with chocolates and a jug, which Mum treasured and promised to see us some time in the future. An Army lorry came to collect them, they climbed aboard and their journey to 'somewhere in France' had commenced. They looked determined and vowed to give Hitler a 'Good Hiding'. We knew we would probably never see them again and our house which was used as a billet for so many months seemed so empty. Our log fire was still blazing and 'Mick ran all over the place looking for his pals then he laid down in front of the blazing fire and wept and wept. He cried his eyes out. He felt so lonely - didn't we all!

Many months later in late May we heard on the Radio the shock news of the evacuation of the British Army at Dunkirk, hundreds of British warships and other vessels under constant attack rescued about 330,000 men from the beaches and brought them to the safety of our Island. Hitler announced the defeat of his enemies and his troops conquered Belgium, Holland and France. Italy declared war on Great Britain and hostilities in France ended in late June. Two of the soldiers billeted with us came to see us. Sadly several of the boys lost their lives in France and Dunkirk. One of the fellows who visited us said that as he ran along the beach to save his life prior to boarding one of the vessels to return to England, he remembered Mum's departing words urging him to look to the Lord above for strength, and he did this, as he needed all his courage and strength at this time of defeat for Great Britain.

Chapter Three

Our 'Private School'
(Lessons in our home)

For many months at the commencement of the war all schools in Gosport were closed and the schools evacuated and most school buildings had been taken over as ARP and First Aid Centres. 'ARP?' Well this stands for Air Raid Precautions. The authorities organised these centres and the Home Guard and Women's Voluntary Service were set up. Members of the public volunteered for duty in a capacity to suit their abilities. Many men and women were too old to be called for active service in one of the Armed Forces. I believe the maximum age was forty-one, but these people would act in a civilian capacity to protect our town. It was the job of an ARP Warden, who was supplied with a tin hat and uniform, to ensure that our 'Blackout' was adequate. It is not an easy task to completely black out the light from a house and ensure that not even a crack of light can be seen from outside the house. Most people obtained plywood and painted it black and affixed the wood to the windows. Others brought black material and made

28

heavy curtains and in addition all lights were dimmed. Even a fire in a room with no blackout would not be allowed. In some cases folk would blackout their main rooms and if they required to use a non-blacked out room would feel their way around in the dark. Car and bicycle lights were dimmed and also torch lights. It was said that from the air even the faintest light could be detected, and no-one wanted to give the Germans any help in bombing our town. Also in case of invasion all road signs indicating names of places were blocked out - I feel that if the Germans invaded, they would soon find their way around, even though the town indicator signs had been obliterated.

The Air Raid Wardens would also endeavour to see that everyone had taken shelter, and we were strongly advised to go to our shelters or stay indoors in the event of an air raid. Public Air Raid shelters were built near shopping centres and on open spaces. If we should see any low flying aircraft we should take cover, even if the siren had not sounded, and this advice was to prove very important to us in the months to come.

During the war no church bells were to be rung and we were informed that in the event of invasion the bells would ring out and this would be a sign that the Germans had landed in our country.

Other precautions to be taken included the avoidance of Careless Talk and the posters 'Careless Talk Cost Lives' could be seen everywhere. For instance, say a husband or brother was on leave, he must be careful what information he divulged concerning the action he had been involved in, or any training or plans for future action as there may be spies about and friends or relations may inadvertently put the country at risk by gossiping about Service movements.

All public transport was dimly lit and the windows of the buses were covered with a kind of adhesive netting to avoid the glass splintering in the event of an explosion.

We were issued with Gas Masks during the 1938 Crisis and these were black, made of rubber and covered the whole face. There was a see-through section for the eyes. These gas masks were issued in regulation cardboard boxes and we were encouraged to carry them with us everywhere. The shops soon had on display attractive leather or canvas containers for the gas masks, some incorporated a handbag, and, despite the war, everyone tried to look smart. At first we would not venture outside without the gas mask, but as time passed by we all became careless and left our 'face masks' as they were called, at home.

I must return to the closing of the schools and of course most of the children in the area had been evacuated. There were a few children like Eileen and myself who for one reason or another had returned home, and other children had remained home prior to the outbreak of war when the evacuation was arranged. The school authorities held a meeting of parents as the lack of education for the children was a matter of growing concern. When school buildings were not available the parents were asked to 'open their homes as schools' and teachers would be available to take the classes. I remember that my mother readily agreed to allow a class to be held at our home every morning and Eileen, together with about ten of her classmates, sharpened their pencils and wits to commence learning and make up for lost time. A very pleasant lady teacher called every day and our 'Private School' had started. I attended a similar class in a neighbour's house and after a time 'my' class was held at our home. It was a very commendable effort on the part of the teachers, parents and students and we all benefited from the lessons. After a considerable time the schools started to re-open and Eileen eventually wore her new school uniform and started the new school she should have attended at the beginning of September 1939. My school remained closed all the War as it was a vital First Aid and ARP Centre - completely sandbagged on the outside. Prior to the war the authorities started building a new school near my home and this was one building which was treated as a priority and the builders were allowed to finish the building of the school. I was in the first class to attend the new school, and I must say, upon reflection, that the number of teachers was totally inadequate. I was ten years old at the time and often had to 'stand in' for the teacher when the younger children were reading.

The grounds of the school apart from the pitch playground were still rough ground, and, of course, we were well equipped with Air Raid Shelters. A nearby school was bombed and that school amalgamated with our school. For a considerable part of the day we had 'gardening' as a lesson and we were each given a plot of rough ground to cultivate, we grew vegetables and flowers. The time of the 'Battle of Britain' was fast approaching, we had many daylight air raids and the children spent most of the school hours in the air raid shelters, where we all had a great deal of fun. At this time sweets were in short supply. I believe it was before the rationing so they were not fairly distributed in the shops. During the summer months the pitch playground started to melt and the children discovered that they could scoop up a piece of the playground and it tasted very sweet and nice and was a substitute for sweets and also free.

Every day we would have to sit in the classroom for about ten minutes with our gas masks on, and I have no doubt that very little studying was achieved during these uncomfortable minutes. The eye piece would get steamed up and we felt that we could not breathe.

Despite the ever constant air raids when we dodged our lessons I very much enjoyed my few months at this brand new school. Sadly, a few of my school mates and a teacher were killed by enemy action during the time I was attending the school.

About this time on 1st July 1941 our Channel Islands were occupied by Germany and the Battle of Britain commenced.

Chapter Four

The Battle of Britain
(The ups and downs of life during the 1940's)

During the summer months of 1940 my home town suffered many daytime raids and the terrible drone of an enemy bomber together with gunfire from our Army Artillery were familiar sounds to my young ears. Prior to the war, air raid shelters were installed for all residents who chose to have them. They were such ugly little shelters made of corrugated iron and installed in a big hole dug in the garden of the house. Many people nicknamed them 'Dugouts' for about four foot of the shelter was underground and the roof of the shelter rose over the surface of the ground in a dome shape. Some people tried to plant grass and flowers on the roof of the shelter in an effort to make these little monstrosities more attractive. Householders would try to make the inside more habitable by putting canvas, carpet or mats on the ground and installing seats or bunks, and chose to have an 'Anderson' shelter installed in their gardens as they were so unsure of what the future had in store for us during these troubled times. Others said that

'Come and see our damage and give to our Spitfire fund'.

they would prefer to stay indoors in case of a raid and perhaps take shelter under a big table or bed. The safest and strongest place in the average house is the area under the staircase, and often, a bombed building would be demolished except for the staircase. We were fortunate as we had a very large cupboard under the stairs which would be adequate for us to shelter in should the need arise.

Our neighbours were very kind to us and one lady suggested that we should use her shelter in the garden of her house should there be a raid, this would protect us and also keep her company. We had no idea what would happen in the coming years and decided to take advantage of her kind offer. We had several false alarms. I mean the Air Raid siren sounded but there was no action, but despite this we took cover in the neighbour's shelter. One sunny afternoon Mum was hanging out the washing on the clothes line in the garden and the Air Raid siren sounded. Mum ushered Eileen and I to the shelter but decided to finish what she was doing. It is often most inconvenient to stop whatever one is doing to run to the shelter, especially if there is no visible sign of the enemy. A kind old Air Raid Warden who had been supplied with a tin hat and uniform ran around blowing his whistle, and when he saw my mother in the garden yelled to her to hurry up and take cover. On this occasion the enemy aircraft flew low over our house and the new type of fighter plane called the Spitfire intercepted and there was what the locals called

'A Dog Fight' in the air. It was our first real air raid and we soon heard the clatter of tiles from someone's roof. We were horrified to see that there was a big hole in our roof. It had been caused by a shell or piece of shrapnel not a bomb. All the neighbours gathered at our house to inspect the damage but none of us could find the piece of shell/shrapnel which had caused the damage to our roof. A little later on the washing was dry on the line and Mum started to bring it indoors for ironing. In one article of underclothing she found a piece of shell - what a souvenir. We were the first house to my knowledge to be damaged in Gosport by enemy action!

At this time all efforts were being directed to providing sufficient ammunition, tanks, guns, ships and Spitfires and the Mayor of Gosport had started a fund to raise £6,000, which was a lot of money at the time, so that the residents could provide enough money to buy their own Spitfire. Eileen and I were members of the Girl Guides and as my mother was on friendly terms with a well known Councillor and his wife at the time who were organising the fund on behalf of the Mayor, we were 'roped in' to make house to house collections. We spent all our time calling at every house in Elson, Brockhurst and Forton and it sometimes took quite a lot of courage to knock on people's doors to ask for money for our Spitfire Fund Box. We were often jokingly told that the person had already given sufficient money to buy their own Spitfire. We

Eileen and Joan in their Girl Guide uniforms where
we collected for the mayor of
Gosport's Spitfire Fund

were so successful in our little Girl Guide uniforms we had a 'special mention' in the Portsmouth Evening News.

On the day of the air raid when we received the first damage known to us and our neighbours, people from all over Gosport called to look at the damage and we had crowds walking up and down our back alley way looking at our damaged roof. Eileen and I realised what an opportunity we had to raise money and asked the sightseers to contribute to our Spitfire Fund Box. Needless to say, we collected a lot of money.

Following this air raid we were to encounter the might of the German Air Force and day after day we heard the familiar sound of the siren, sometimes six or seven times a day. Each time we ran to the shelter and it was beginning to feel like a second home to us. By this time, many properties in our area were very badly damaged and it was like living through a kind of hell. Air fights were very common sights and we often saw German and English pilots and crews parachuting from their planes following one of these fights.

One day, during the long summer, Eileen and Mum went to Portsmouth and I attended school. During the day there was a terrible air raid and Eileen and Mum took shelter in a Public Shelter near Victoria Park. During the air raid an air battle took place and the glorious Spitfires attacked the unwelcome intruders. Some pilots parachuted from their planes to safety and one of the men in the shelter could not resist, despite warnings, watching, and stood outside the shelter. Sadly, a piece of shrapnel hit him, and the emergency services took him to the nearest hospital. The very next day the shelter received a direct hit and about fifty people were killed. When Mum visited the area the following week, the shelter had been completely demolished.

My family were a long time returning home on this occasion, and I remember feeling very worried and feared the worst, for I hated to think that I might be left alone in the world.

The kind lady who allowed us to use her shelter decided she could not stand the bombing anymore and she evacuated to be with her family in the country, but we continued to use the shelter together with some other neighbours. After what seemed many months of raids, damaged property, air fights, deaths of friends, food rationing and no news of Dad, we started to get night-time raids which were even worse than the daylight raids. One night the siren sounded and I dressed as quickly as I could in the dark and rushed to the shelter. Eileen and Mum accompanied me and with another lady neighbour we settled down to a night in the shelter. It seemed so quiet. Suddenly a noise was heard which was far more frightening than the whistle of a bomb or gunfire. It was the dreaded, and I mean dreaded, sound of the Church Bells. This was the sign that an invasion had started. I was petrified, I could at this stage hear just a few screams and I guess I was not the only frightened person about. Even the word German sent a cold chill up my spine and the thought of us being invaded was simply horrifying. I know Eileen felt the same but my mother and the lady neighbour showed no sign of fear. The neighbour grabbed a heavy broom and Mum got our pitchfork and said 'God help any German who comes near us.' She no doubt remembered dear old Winston's words 'We will fight them on the beaches...WE WILL NEVER SURRENDER.'

I crouched down in my bunk and hid under a blanket. I know I am a coward. Unlike any other raid, I mean a normal raid with gunfire and bombs, it was all so very quiet. Suddenly, we heard footsteps approaching the shelter; left right left right. Was it a German? I thought my end had come - help! I'm too young to die.

A voice in English yelled out 'Are you alright in there?' It was the friendly ARP warden who was visiting all the shelters. I then did what all brave or cowardly little girls should do in an emergency - I went to sleep. I was too tired and too young to worry!

The next morning nothing happened - no Germans - no invasion - and several news bulletins insisted that it was a false alarm - I wonder! At this time my father was still away at sea. On his return home he told us that several German ships had left France for England, presumably to invade us, there was a battle involving his ship and other

RN Ships and the German attempt was abandoned.

Following this terrifying experience we continued to run for shelter everytime there was an air raid, and one night a neighbour in the shelter was taken very ill. My mother and the kind lady neighbour who had grabbed the broom at the time of the invasion, rendered first aid. My mother was so concerned she forgot the bombing and ordered Eileen and I out of the shelter and back to the house - and we never ever returned to the little shelter in our neighbour's garden.

At this time my mother caught a severe chill and had shingles very badly, and it fell on Eileen and I to try to nurse her back to health. Everyone felt very low. Eileen was a brick, she did all the shopping and cooked us lovely meals and soon became a very efficient little wartime cook. I made every effort to keep the house clean and tidy and helped to nurse Mum who soon recovered. However, the illness had taken its toll and winter was approaching. We decided to take shelter indoors under the stairs in future and if we were going to die at least it would be in comfort. We placed cushions, blankets and a torch in the cupboard under the stairs in readiness for the many many nights to be spent in that big cupboard.

The black days of war seemed to loom heavy. Our British Army had been defeated in France in the June and our boys had to run for their very lives along the beaches at Dunkirk. Our Navy was very valiant but many ships had been lost or damaged, including the Royal Oak, and later the Hood. Our Air Force were magnificent during the Battle of Britain and against overwhelming odds this had been won. Nearly all of Europe had been occupied including Norway and Denmark and in October the Germans invaded Roumania. The Cathedral town of Coventry had been under very heavy attack and the cathedral (apart from the altar) had been destroyed. All young men and women were serving in the forces (unless they were in some vital work). Some women joined the Women's Voluntary Services and looked most attractive in their green uniforms. First Aiders and Air Raid Wardens and Home Guard were all in uniform. Eileen and I joined the Girl Guides and we were in uniform, and the only person who did not wear a uniform was my dear Mum!

A lot of people felt like us and realised they could not survive the winter nights in a shelter in the garden. Most people brought their beds downstairs to the safest part of the house and we all dug our heels in for another wartime Christmas. One night I completely slept through an air raid and, in the morning, I was sad to see from the upstairs window of our house, that a road away two houses had received two hits with high explosive bombs. In one house the family of four were in the shelter and this received a direct hit. All perished except a little girl. If they had been in the house they would have survived. Their four neighbours took shelter indoors and their house received a direct hit and they all perished except for the father. Their shelter in the garden, which was empty, would have saved them.

I don't think anyone who experienced the war in England was ever hungry, but essential foods were rationed and it was necessary for us all to be issued with a ration book and one had to register with a grocer who would supply all the groceries which were on ration. For example, tea, sugar, cheese, butter, margarine and meat were rationed. The shops were beginning to look empty at times and it was impossible to buy such items as eggs, cakes chocolate biscuits, alcoholic drinks, some tinned food, dried fruit, fresh fruit such as oranges, lemons, grapefruit. A new type of restaurant was opened called 'The British Restaurant' and a very cheap meal could be purchased to help supplement our diet. I think it cost 1/- (5p in decimal money) Mum stocked up with tea, sugar and tinned foods etc. prior to the outbreak of war, but we all took about three teaspoonfuls of sugar in our tea and our stocks were beginning to dwindle. One day my Aunt from Portsmouth visited us and she had run out of sugar and so went without. She said 'if you can go without sugar completely for a fortnight you will never need to take sugar again in hot drinks.' Through necessity we tried this and drank our tea without sugar and it tasted like poison to me. However, we persevered and I can state that, in my case, I have never taken sugar in any hot drink since that day nearly sixty years ago! Our ration of cheese was laughable, just about a square inch which one could eat in one mouthful. Incidentally, I don't think coffee was rationed.

When my father returned from sea he said that the lads on board used to pool their sweet rations so that fellows with children could take home some sweets. We were always glad to see daddy come home particularly as he always brought a case filled with chocolate and sweets. How we all indulged!

Sometimes when jam was short Mum would cook runner beans (grown in the garden) or carrots and we would have 'carrot' jam and spread the mashed vegetable on our bread. During the war years bread was not rationed, but following the cessation of hostilities it was found necessary to ration bread and the other commodities remained on ration right up to 1952 and beyond.

On 2nd June of the next year a new kind of rationing was introduced called 'points rationing' and these points enabled us to purchase certain groceries which had in some cases been in short supply from any grocer. I think some tinned food was on this points rationing system, and also biscuits, dried fruit etc.

In December of 1941 clothing rationing was introduced and this caused us some annoyance as the number of new clothes we could have was severely restricted. As far as I can remember every item of clothing was rationed including shoes, and most of our clothing coupons were required for our school uniforms.

Eileen and I were very keen on swimming and the open air pool was a favourite meeting place for us and our friends. In addition we belonged to the Bridgemary Section of the Girl Guides and met at an old Church (long since demolished). The church was a very pretty country church and its grounds ran down to the shore of the harbour. At low tide it was very muddy but at high tide suitable for splashing about in the water. Swimming was also popular for children at Hardway (an area near us on the shores of Portsmouth Harbour) and we also swam in Haslar Creek at Gosport Park. The lovely clean shingle beaches at Stokes Bay and our favourite spot Haslar Sea Wall were closed to the public, although the beach at Lee-on-the-Solent (about 2½ miles from home) was open for the public's use. Unfortunately the very attractive pier at Lee-on-the Solent, and the one at Stokes Bay, were damaged, so that they could not be used in the case of invasion by the enemy, and these piers have never been replaced. One article of clothing we could not purchase was a swimsuit, so my dear aunt Lilian used her own clothing coupons to purchase some wool and knitted us a costume each. When the costumes were completed they fitted us quite nicely, but when we entered the water they stretched a lot and we felt very uncomfortable, especially climbing out of the swimming pool with a very soggy swim suit. In addition rubber was in short supply and despite all our efforts we could not find a shop with any old stock swimming caps.

In those days every one wore a covering over their heads when swimming. They say every problem has a solution so Mum bought some black shiny semi waterproof blackout material and made us a little round hat each, the outside was gathered with elastic to fit the head. Needless to say, when we dived in the water this head covering would come off - very unsatisfactory - especially with an over-stretched swimming costume.

During the air raids it sometimes transpired that a bomb would be dropped and, for some mechanical reason, it would remain unexploded. In addition, lots of bombs missed the towns and fell in the harbour and were lodged in the mud. An uncle of mine was a Seaman prior to Dunkirk when his boats were confiscated to save the lives of the soldiers who were trapped on the beach at Dunkirk. He continued his livelihood as an employee of HM Dockyard and because of his seamanship abilities, captained small boats in the Harbour and carried passengers and goods from one section of the Harbour to another. One morning Eileen and I heard a terrific explosion and guessed that an unexploded bomb had blown up. We were so sad to learn that this favourite Uncle of ours had hit an unexploded bomb or mine whilst acting as Captain of a small boat in the Harbour. His body was the only one found in one piece and my mother and aunt were required to identify him.

As 1940 was drawing to a close we all listened

intently to the News on the Radio and Big Ben chiming was a reassuring sound.

We had lived through the 'Battle of Britain' what was in store for us next? Mr Churchill in a very stirring speech promised us 'Nothing but, blood tears, toil and sweat'.

Chapter Five

Making a Cake
(Memories of a Blitz on 10th January 1941)

On the last day of December 1940 I was just eleven years old and my interests were beginning to widen. I was very keen on roller skating and I think I was a very contented child.

My mother had bought me a little book of autographs. It was the craze at the time to obtain autographs from friends and they usually wrote a little verse in the book. I asked my mother to be the first to write in the book and she wrote the verse:-

'Welcome nineteen forty one
I hope by next year the War is done'.

I thought the War could not possibly last much longer and I personally had no idea how serious the position was for our country.

I was also acquiring another interest - cooking - or should I say Eileen was learning how to cook cakes at school and wanted to practise at home. That January was very cold, and in the early evening of the 10th January it was already freezing. Despite this we were very cosy at home and Mum said that Eileen and I could 'have a go' at making a cake. Eileen was 'in charge' and weighed out the ingredients on the new scales which Mum had bought. I remember flour being one of the ingredients (this was not rationed) and margarine, sugar (rationed) and powdered egg. In case you don't know, it was impossible to purchase eggs in this locality but powdered eggs and powdered milk could be purchased (dehydrated eggs in powder form which was mixed with water and used as a substitute for eggs). Mum suggested putting some cocoa into the cake to make a 'chocolate cake', we had nothing else in the house for the cake and dried fruit such as sultanas were unobtainable. Eileen put all the weighed ingredients into a big yellow bowl and it was my job to mix the soggy ingredients by hand. We then put the mixture into a big tin and lit the gas oven. We sat down in our dining room and started to listen to the radio. In those days television was unknown to most people. At about 7 pm the all too familiar sound of the siren started wailing. This siren gave warning that enemy aircraft had been spotted.

During bad air raids Mum insisted that Eileen and I should sit in the big cupboard under the stairs. We did not have an air raid shelter in the garden and in any case it was freezing cold that January evening. Sometimes the air raid warning siren sounded and nothing seemed to happen, presumably the German planes were flying over Gosport to reconnoitre or perhaps bomb another

49

town. On this particular evening we soon realised that we were going to have a noisy time. Eileen and I sat in the cupboard under the stairs and in accordance with our usual practice, we turned off the oven gas and also switched the electricity and gas off at the mains in case of a direct hit. Mum was very brave during the whole of the war and stood just outside the cupboard, sometimes standing in the doorway on hearing the whistle which can be heard as a bomb is falling to earth to damage our nice little town.

It was a terrible night. The Army's artillery thundered in an effort to stop the enemy intruders, gunfire, bombs falling, loud explosions shaking the whole house, flashes in the sky, search lights. Flares kept flashing, and enemy bombers kept diving in an effort to hit special targets, presumably Naval Ships in the Harbour, the Dockyard or one of the many Service Establishments. I think I was too young to be scared and somehow I knew I would survive together with my beloved family. However, I had experienced all the Battle of Britain air raids but I knew this particular Blitz was indeed a very severe raid. At one time a long long whistle was heard; it seemed endless and we awaited the impact of the bomb. The whole house lifted and returned to earth. Mum usually opened all windows and doors to allow any blast to go through the house and to try to save our windows. On this particular occasion all open doors and windows slammed and we were in utter darkness. A landmine had fallen quite near us and many houses were badly damaged.

During an air raid, especially one in the night, there was always an eerie feeling, sometimes in between the gunfire and bombs it seemed very quiet, then perhaps an Ambulance, Police Car or despatch rider, on a noisy motor-cycle, could be heard. We often noticed that after hearing the depatch rider the all clear would sound. After what seemed a lifetime to me, but in fact must have been about three hours, we heard the despatch rider and shortly after the long even siren could be heard signifying the 'All Clear', enemy planes have passed.

During the raid Mum and some of the neighbours were amazed to notice that a new type of bomb was being dropped, 'An Incendiary Bomb' and if a person was quick enough, as the bomb did not explode straight away, the incendiary bomb could be smothered with sand (always kept handy) and thus the damage by fire would be minimized.

Mum soon bundled two tired little girls into bed and we were just dropping off to sleep when the Siren went again. At first Mum said 'forget it - stay in bed' but we soon got up when the bombs started falling again. I believe I eventually fell asleep, as I had done on many occasions before 'under the stairs'. Obviously, we made ourselves as comfortable as possible with cushions and blankets. When the 'All Clear' sounded again Eileen and I plucked up courage to take a look outside from an upstairs window. I have already said that we could see the Guildhall at Portsmouth from our house. As long as I live I shall never forget the sight which befell my eyes. The whole area was red and ablaze. It looked as though there would be nothing at all left of our beloved Portsmouth, and of course, there were fires all over Gosport which was very badly damaged. It was like being in the midst of a blazing inferno. We thought no-one could have survived in Portsmouth and knew that we were lucky to be alive, and we had lived through the worst blitz we had experienced of the War.

During the time of the Blitzes a certain comradeship developed and the neighbours were much more friendly. Mum would often let friends and neighbours have sugar or tea as some people found it impossible to manage on their rations. Some of the men who lived along the road would pop in to see if we were OK especially during or after a bad air raid. Often following a night raid neighbours would visit us for breakfast and we would exchange snippets of news about the damage in the town and also try to comfort each other. It did not take us long on the morning of 11th January, to realise that life would not be back to normal as we knew it for some time. For example, there was no gas or electricity, for the Gasometers in Forton Road had been hit and were smouldering for about three weeks after. Of course Mum soon lit a nice fire and we managed to heat up some water on the fire for a wash and breakfast.

At the time we had quite a few relations living in Portsmouth, and, in particular, my grandfather and his daughter my auntie Hilda lived in Southsea. My grandfather was very old in his eighties and none of us had a telephone. Not many people did in those days, in any case all telephones were out of action following the devastation. I can remember my mother saying 'I think we had better go to Southsea to see if your grandfather is still alive.' Mum could not go there alone and leave us, and we had long before decided that we wanted to stick together and, if anything happened, we wanted to 'go together'.

I can't remember if any of the buses were running in Gosport but I do remember noticing that our familiar High Street was very badly damaged. Some of the shops had been demolished; no windows in any shops, other businesses badly damaged bravely showed the sign 'business as usual'.

The quickest way to reach Portsmouth from Gosport Town is by ferry boat across the narrow Portsmouth Harbour and in 1941 there were two services operating. One ferry boat went from the Pontoon at Gosport to the Hard at Portsea (near Portsmouth Dockyard), this service is still in operation. The other ferry boat served the Old Portsmouth area. There was also a car ferry which operated on chains from Gosport to Old Portsmouth. Mum decided it best to take the Ferry from Gosport to Old Portsmouth. Everywhere along Broad Street and High Street was damaged. It was very smoky and some buildings were still on fire or smouldering. Men were digging to try to save people trapped in the basement of some buildings and ambulances, police and fire engines were everywhere. The work of these men and women was magnificent. Fire fighters made courageous attempts to save the City. The ground was all wet from leaking hose pipes and we clambered over these to proceed to Southsea. Obviously no buses were running so we had to walk. I can still remember the uncanny feeling seeing a house so recently bombed and sometimes the roof and the side of the house would be in a big heap alongside an unsafe wall. On this wall one could often see a picture on the wall or a clock which was still going. Police and Ambulance and First Aiders, Civilians and Service men were all helping to clear the debris and I saw some bodies being carried from the devastation. Under no circumstances, would we have been allowed along the road but for the fact that we had to visit Southsea to see if my grandfather was OK, and there was no other way to ascertain this information.

My mother and Eileen and I started to walk along the High Street near St. George's Court and there were lots of damaged houses with no doors or windows and these were of course empty. There had been no siren so we had no reason to suppose that we should take cover. A plane flew low over the devastated area. I looked up and saw the black cross which indicated it was an enemy aircraft. We heard some shots and realised that the enemy plane was machine gunning us. It was horrifying. I felt I was 'too young to die.' We have never moved so fast either before or since. We literally flew into one of the empty houses with no door or windows and took refuge under a table until the danger had passed. I am unaware if any of the men working in this area were killed or injured. After this fright we continued our walk to Southsea and wondered if our relations were still alive and dreaded what we would see as we approached their home.

Grandfather's house was quite badly damaged but we were so relieved that although badly shaken, our relations were alright.

Talk about In the Bleak Midwinter. During the next few weeks, and I can't remember if it was two or three weeks, we had to survive without gas or electricity during the darkest and coldest weeks of winter. Some folk were unfortunate as they ran out of fuel, but we were well stocked with coal and coke and logs and Mum kept the cheerful fire going. I can remember her trying to cook a roast dinner on the open fire. We sat during the long evenings with a candle light and the glow from the fire and swapped stories and Mum continued to give us a drop of Taragona wine every evening. The gasometers in Forton Road were still smouldering and I thought life would never return to normal. Several of the children at my school were killed and we were very saddened to hear stories of families who had lost everything. An Aunt's sister was buried alive under the debris of her house in Portsmouth and spent many months in hospital, her husband was killed. We were so thankful to be alive but there was always the fear that my father, who was on active service in *HMS Aurora,* would be lost at sea. I have no doubt that he heard the news about the terrible blitz on Portsmouth and Gosport and he was equally worried about us.

After several weeks the gas and electricity was reinstated - Mum went to the oven to prepare a decent meal for us and guess what! The chocolate cake we made on the 10th January, the night of the blitz was still there. All three of us had completely forgotten it. It was partially cooked, but the inside was completely sunken like the crater of a volcano. It was many years before I made another cake!

My Uncle Jack Cottrell who was a seafaring man, had his boats confiscated at the time of Dunkirk and so he took employment with the Auxiliary Fire Service. He told of his dreadful experiences on the night of the blitz in Portsmouth. All over the City there were big tanks or reservoirs full of water to be used by firemen in case of need. When the incendiary bombs fell little was known of them or the best way to deal with them. Unfortunately, all the tanks of water were frozen solid and the firemen could not get water to put out the fires. This may be the reason why so many buildings were destroyed by fire.

Chapter Six

I have an Examination Tomorrow
(*Memories of the Blitz on 10th March 1941*)

Following the terrible Blitz of the 10th January we continued to be plagued with Air Raids, although there was little damage. If the air raid was not directed at our area we could hear the gunfire in the distance and flashes and flares in the sky. I remember one occasion when Southampton was badly bombed and we knew an area west of Gosport was being bombarded and we sympathised with the residents.

On the 10th February we experienced a not too serious Air Raid. Some people used to listen on the Radio to Lord Joyce, more commonly known as Lord Haw Haw. He was an English Lord who was in the employ of Germany. Although he had a cultured voice there was a terrible sneer in the voice which could be detected. His propaganda programme was designed to break the morale of the British people - what a hope! As Sir Winston Churchill said in one of his memorable speeches 'Hitler thought he would ring the British neck like a chicken'. Some chicken! Some neck! Everyone listened to Lord Haw Haw but he was not taken seriously and he was a source of amusement to us and we mimicked him, mainly to keep up our spirits. Just prior to the War several old Victorian and Georgian houses at the foot of the High Street were demolished in order to modernise the town. I remember the houses very well as some friends of ours lived in an upstairs flat in one of the properties from which there was a good view over the Harbour. A lovely new modern store was being built on the site of the old houses and this store was called Littlewoods. I suppose it was so near completion the authorities decided to allow it to be completed, otherwise unfinished property would soon become derelict. The same position ensued with my new school which was not completed at the commencement of the war. Obviously no new building took place other than the construction of buildings required for War needs. For example, factories; canteens for service men, Service establishments. To return to the new store in Gosport, it certainly brightened the area and all the residents were keen to visit Littlewoods which was conveniently situated next to Woolworths. Both stores are still there.

Just prior to the 10th March Lord Haw Haw stated that a new store had opened in High Street, Gosport, and the German bombers would soon knock it down; a slight cause for alarm to know that the Germans were watching our every day life. We wondered if they knew that there were some

Naval ships in Portsmouth harbour. Were their spies everywhere? Was there Careless Talk?

On the 11th March I was due to take an examination to allow me to become a student at the Secondary School (or Grammar School). The children who attended this school wore attractive dark green uniforms. However, there was one big snag - the school was still evacuated to Eastleigh I believe. If I passed the examination (more recently called eleven plus) I would have to be evacuated again and this time I would have to go alone without Eileen. Ugh! Not a very inviting thought. There was an alternative. One could opt out of the chance to attend the Grammar School and attend the Central School which was now open, and one would receive a satisfactory commercial education. The school uniform of navy blue was very smart, and despite all the clothing coupon rationing students were required to wear the uniform at all times when at school, and in addition, in winter, a navy blue coat or gaberdine mack with the navy blue velour hat, and a white panama hat in the summer with navy blue blazer. I was not particularly concerned about the examination. I never considered myself 'clever' but at the same time had no difficulty whatsoever with my studies. I was quite keen to attend the Central School and I had already learned a little French from Eileen and often sat with her when she undertook her homework. I was hoping to have an early night on the 10th March in order to have a good little clear brain for the examination the following day.

At this time my Dad came home. He did not talk much to Eileen and I about his 'active service' with the Royal Navy. We knew that his cruiser, the *Aurora,* had been damaged in enemy action and was being repaired, and the Naval Authorities had taken this opportunity to give the lads shore leave. During the week we had an air raid every night and he jokingly said he would be glad to get back to sea for some peace and quiet. Although my parents never showed concern, I know they must have felt some comfort that we were all together during these dark days.

On the evening of the 10th March - guess what? The sirens sounded again and upon the sound of bombs dropping Eileen and I were quickly ushered to the cupboard under the stairs. I sat trying to shuffle cards as quickly as Dad could. This was my main ambition at the time. This was Dad's first experience of a very bad blitz and it seemed the bombs were dropping all night - a noise very familiar to us now. As with the 10th January Blitz, in addition to landmines, and high explosive bombs, many incendiary bombs were dropped. Our house was the end house with a little field next to us and being quite near the harbour and exposed it always seemed very windy, and sometimes the wind would blow down the chimney and cause a down draught. For this reason my parents had a cowl placed on the chimney which would rotate in the wind, quite a common sight at the time.

On this night the moon was very bright and of

course, the ground barrage was busy trying to defend the Port. The bombers dived low and there were showers and showers of incendiary bombs. The fire fighters did a magnificent job trying to control the many fires, and official sources stated that the raids continued for seven hours and there were many homeless people.

During this evening there was an extra noisy explosion and the whole house shook and we all knew that we had been hit.

Our lovely clean cosy dining room was one mass of soot. Everything was black. What had happened? We were all shaky but uninjured. Dad and Mum rushed out of the house to see what damage had occurred. Providence had saved us. The incendiary bomb had hit the chimney cowl and the cowl from the impact swung the bomb on to the little field next to our house. My parents smothered the bomb with sand and earth to prevent it spreading and Dad climbed up to the roof loft and dealt with another incendiary bomb thus saving our house from burning. Obviously the chimney and roof were damaged, but we could still live in the house. Our neighbours all suffered similar damage and every house in the Avenue was damaged as far as I know. Some quite serious damage occurred from fires. Mercifully lots of bombs went into the Harbour. I had the feeling that there could not be many buildings standing in Portsmouth.

After an uncomfortable night under the stairs I went to school to take my examination the next morning. No time for pre-examination nerves. I was just glad we were all alive and together. Adolf Hitler had tried to destroy the rest of Gosport and Portsmouth with this major blitz and in some ways he nearly succeeded. Gosport took a terrible battering and poor old Portsmouth - oh dear. The popular shopping centre in Commercial Road had been obliterated. Palmerston Road and Osborne Road flattened, Harbour Station damaged, the Dockyard damaged and many many houses in Gosport and Portsmouth either damaged or destroyed.

Winston Churchill inspired us all, even me, and we were determined to keep on to the end of the road whatever happened. No German was going to take our country from us! By the way, I passed the examination and chose to attend the Central School as I was not prepared to leave home again and be evacuated. Once in a lifetime is enough for that. Many teachers thought this was a foolish decision on my part - who cares - I was alive!

Oh! I forgot to mention that our lovely new store in the High Street remained standing, possibly it was damaged.

I have not paid tribute to the authorities who were always on hand with ambulances, fire engines and risked all to save lives. At the time of the blitzes and air raids I was too young to realise what sacrifices were being made for our very existence. I will now pay tribute to the brave men and women in the civilian services who kept my home town going.

Chapter Seven

Our Visit to Buckingham Palace
(Story of the exploits and brilliant Naval Battle of HMS Aurora)

My father served in the Royal Navy on HMS Aurora a 5270 ton Cruiser which was commissioned in 1937 the day we entered our new house. Thus, our house is called Aurora. As a child I was unaware of my father's bravery and the exploits of the Cruiser Aurora. I knew he spent some time in Spitzbergen which is about 560 miles from the North Pole and also there was plenty of action in the Mediterranean Sea. I have just been looking through some of his papers and discovered further details of his exploits. The Cruiser Aurora was nicknamed The Silver Phantom and also The Shadow by the Italian Press.

There was one story Dad used to tell. It took place in the Spring of 1940, at the time the German Army had occupied Norway. The port of Narvik, which controlled the North Sea Coast, was under occupation. On a hill overlooking the Port the German flag was flying, and this annoyed the British ships which constantly bombarded the port.

The lads on the Cruiser asked the Captain for permission to try to shoot the flag down but Captain Agnew refused this permission on the grounds that ammunition was short. Following a day's heavy bombardment by the British Navy there was one round of ammunition left in one gun and the Captain said it would be OK to fire this one round in an effort to hit the flagstaff. Everything was checked and from a distance of 5300 yards the flagstaff was hit amidst cheers from the ship's crew.

My father was known as 'guns' and was responsible for the gunnery machinery. There was a Gunnery Officer in charge who later became First Sea Lord. The *Aurora* was renowned for the excellence of her gunnery, no doubt due to expert training prior to the war.

Details of action my father was involved in have just been found by me amongst his papers. Some of the action is given as follows:-

Spitzbergen Summer 1941 -
12 merchant vessels and trawlers captured.

| Baffin Bay - | German supply ship 20,000 tons destroyed 2 subs destroyed |
| Svaerholthaven | North Cape Norway - 71 degrees N 27 degrees E 1 Cruiser, 1 Destroyer 1 Convey vessel, 1 Trawler and 2 subs destroyed |

Benghazi   1 December 1941 - 15
                miles from town
                1 huge merchant vessel at 4 am
Off Tunis - about 6 pm same day
                1 huge oiler 14000 tons and
                Italy's largest destroyer
Taranto -   near Southern Italy Sunday 9
                November 1941 1 am
                10 huge merchant transport
                vessels
                4 destroyers sunk
                1 destroyer badly damaged.

I have found some newspapers dated Monday
10th November 1941 with the headlines 'Taranto
again we sink 10 out of 10,' the ships involved
were the *Aurora, Penelope, Lance* and *Lively*. The
ten merchant vessels were loaded with supplies of
ammunition, troops, fuel and equipment for the
German Afrika Korps under the control of General
Rommel. Apparently his attacks against the British
Army in North Africa had been stopped through
lack of supplies which were urgently required, and
our ships cut Rommel's lifeline. At midnight the
sea was very calm and the moon rose and in the
moonlight the lookouts on the *Aurora* scanned the
seas for the transport vessels. Suddenly, on the
horizon the masts of the vessels could be seen. It
was a brilliant Naval Battle on the part of the British
Royal Navy and it was for this particular battle that
my father was awarded the Distinguished Service

Medal, and a copy of an Admiralty Fleet Order I have just found reads as follows:

'For Gallantry, skill and resolution in a brilliant night action south of Taranto, against odds in which without hurt or loss to the Royal Navy ten enemy supply ships were wholly destroyed, four destroyers sunk and at least one other badly damaged - DSM Sunday 9th November 1941 at 1 am.'

This strangely worded order meant that my father had been decorated for bravery and would be entitled to wear yet another ribbon on his uniform. He had three rows of them as he had served in the 1st World War in the Army. My father was invited to attend an investiture at Buckingham Palace and King George VI was to award the medal. Dad was allowed to bring along two guests to witness the ceremony in one of the big halls at Buckingham Palace. My mother thought it would be a marvellous opportunity for Eileen and I to be Dad's guests. We were very excited and had not fully realised the sacrifice Mum had made on our behalf. At first we thought about wearing our Girl Guide uniforms to the Palace, then Mum decided that despite the War we must all have some new clothes for our visit to the big City.

As with many sisters we were dressed alike, so Mum bought some very attractive blue heavy linen type material and arranged for a local dressmaker to make us a dress each with matching coats. Everyone wore hats in those days so two little hats were purchased and of course we had new shoes

Among those who were decorated by the King at the recent investiture was Chief Ordnance Artificer Bishop, of 79, Albemarle Road, Gosport, who was awarded the D.S.M. He is the only son of Mr J.J. Bishop, of the well-known firm of builders in Southsea. Mr Bishop passed into the Dockyard as an apprentice from Chivers's School, and during the last war served in the Army. Later he joined the Senior Service.

socks and gloves. My mother also had a brand new outfit and the day for the Investiture approached. We travelled to London and stayed one night in the Union Jack Club which is a little hotel near Waterloo Station for Servicemen and their families.

My mother was a lonely figure waiting outside the Palace and Eileen and I entered the big gates that led into the Palace. Maybe I was a little too young to appreciate the importance of the day, but I remember we were ushered into a large beautifully decorated hall and taken to our allotted seats. All the people waiting to be decorated were waiting in another room. They were mainly Servicemen and were presumably given their instructions, and perhaps told what His Majesty was likely to say to them. Then the King appeared and stood on a small platform. He looked very handsome in his Naval Admiral's uniform, but there was no sign of the Queen or the two little Princesses. The King spoke to his brave subjects in turn before proudly pinning on the medal. When it was my father's turn to be decorated the King said a few words to him. His Majesty had obviously followed the exploits of the Silver Phantom with immense interest and at one time during the year 1941 had already boarded the *Aurora* to give encouragement to the crew. At that time my father had also been presented to His Majesty, a great honour indeed.

Outside the Palace there were many reporters and photographers taking pictures of all the brave men and women and they were interested in our story - and Eileen and I were very proud of our Dad.

Shortly after this investiture my father was promoted, and because of his Gunnery expertise, was appointed to the Admiralty at Bath. During 1942 we moved to Bath to be able to see more of my father.

Chapter Eight

Uncle Sam Joins us
*(Events learned from news of the attack on
Pearl Harbour)*

Less than a month after the brilliant Naval victory
in November 1941 there was a news item on the
morning Radio of the 7th December. I believe it
was a Sunday morning and the newsreader had
announced that Pearl Harbour had been attacked
by Japanese planes. This was indeed shocking
news and as a young girl I had never heard of Pearl
Harbour. Of course all newspapers and radios were
giving the people of England the latest news. At
the time Japanese/American relations were at a very
low ebb. Japan had been at war with China for
some time and now wished to acquire further
interests in South East Asia and were prepared to
challenge European and American interests. The
Japanese realised that the superior might of the
Americans might tip the scales against them in any
conquest unless a surprise attack could be arranged.

Pearl Harbour is the main Naval Harbour for
Honolulu on the lovely island of Oahu, one of the
Hawaiian Islands, situated in the middle of the

Pearl Harbour
Remains of USS Arizona

Pacific Ocean, many miles from the coasts of the USA and Japan.

In November a task force of at least 30 warships sailed from Japan. The force included six aircraft carriers. The entire force was hidden because of storms and fog and after taking up a position quite near the Hawaiian Islands the surprise attack was made. The US Pacific fleet was very badly damaged and sadly 2,403 men were killed. In addition over a thousand were wounded. Some of the US Naval ships were salvaged and following repair were later involved in action. In Pearl Harbour today one can see the Arizona Memorial. This is the final resting place for over 1,000 men who lost their lives on the *Arizona* and the *Memorial* spans the sunken battleship. It is a very moving sight to visit this memorial.

Following this attack the United States of America declared war on Japan, Germany and Italy and the Americans were now in the war and 'Uncle Sam' would soon help us free Europe from the unwelcome intruders. Shortly after the attack on Pearl Harbour the Japanese attacked the Philippine Islands, Hong Kong, Singapore, Malaya and soon nearly all the islands in South East Asia had been captured . Our ships, *The Repulse* and *Prince of Wales* were sunk by the Japanese off the coast of Malaya, and the position was very very serious. The British declared war on Japan. The American people were at one time divided as to whether they should be drawn into the war, but were now very resolved that victory should be achieved over Japan and her Axis partners, and in the words of the Japanese Admiral Yamamoto, they had 'awakened a sleeping giant and filled him with remorse'.

The Newsreels on the cinema screen soon showed us pictures of our new enemy, and soon some of the American Servicemen came to England in readiness for the long fight to eventual victory.

At this time I could not imagine life in a peacetime England.

Chapter Nine

We leave the bomb scarred South
*(Main events of the latter part of the war and
how these affected us)*

Following the terrible attack on Pearl Harbour
which brought the Americans into the war, my
father received promotion in the Royal Navy and
was appointed to the Admiralty. At the time part
of the Admiralty had been transferred from London
to the City of Bath. I believe my father reluctantly
left *HMS Aurora* and all the action at sea to take a
desk job at the Admiralty. In fact, I believe the
work involved was pretty important as Dad had
first-hand knowledge of the Action as well as being
a very competent Gunnery Engineer, and had, in
fact received extra pay for some of his inventions
which had been accepted and used by the Royal
Navy.

My father looked so smart in his Naval Officer's
uniform and after some time and discussion, my
parents decided that we should leave our home in
Gosport and rent a house in Bath so that we could
all be together.

By this time it was 1942 and the terrible air raids

had stopped in the Portsmouth area. We did, however, often hear the German Bombers flying overhead to bomb some other unfortunate city. We were saddened to hear stories of the terrible bombing in London when the residents spent the nights in the Underground Railway stations to shelter from the very, very heavy bombing they endured. As already mentioned our shops in Gosport were pretty empty, obviously we were supplied with our rationed goods but not all items of food were rationed. I can remember Eileen and I queuing for about three hours early one morning at a farm for six eggs, quite a luxury, and well worth the long wait. Cake shops used to put artificial cakes in the windows to make a show, but shop-bought cakes were unobtainable at one time, although bread was always plentiful.

All wrought iron railings and gates had been confiscated for the war effort and everyone was just as patriotic. Many wartime songs became popular, such as *The White Cliffs of Dover*, *We'll Meet Again*, *Bless 'em All*, *Quarter Master's Stores*, *A Nightingale Sang in Berkeley Square*. I could go on but the list would be exhaustive. Radio programmes such as ITMA were very popular and the latest sayings from the comedy show were quickly repeated by all - most people tried to keep their 'sense of humour'.

We packed away some of our ornaments and pictures and locked up our House in Gosport, and packed our clothes ready for the journey by rail to

Bath. The Southern Railway steam train took us to Salisbury and we stayed on the train for a long time whilst the engine for the Great Western Railway was attached, and then we made the slow journey from Salisbury to Bath. The train was packed with Servicemen and everywhere were posters such as 'Is your Journey Really Necessary?' and 'Careless Talk costs Lives' also 'Dig for Victory' and big 'V' signs indicated that we were going to achieve victory. As we approached Somerset (Bath was in the County of Somerset in those days) I noticed the lovely green hills, so different from the flat countryside around my home town.

As our train pulled into the main station at Bath all the porters called out 'Bath, Bath Bath' and I noticed their accents were a little different from ours. I was twelve years old and thought that Bath was a beautiful City. All the buildings were of Portland stone and the Georgian properties looked picturesque against the green hills surrounding the City and which form part of the Cotswolds. There is a river running through the area called the Avon, and a unique bridge crosses the Avon at a point in the centre of the city, it is called Pulteney Bridge. It is world renowned as shops are built on the bridge. Bath is also noted for its hot springs and Roman Baths which are the best Roman remains in England. It was very different from Gosport and at times I felt homesick for our cosy little home in the south.

For a time we lived in a rented house a couple of miles from the city centre. The place was a bit drab, despite the fact that the rent was very high. My parents tried to brighten the place by painting the woodwork and emulsioning the walls. At the time it was impossible to buy wall paper. Dad thought it would be a good idea to buy a big map of North Africa and he placed this on the wall of the main room where we had all our meals. Where I sat at the table was very near to the map and I spent a lot of time studying it and thus began to get interested and good at geography. Dad pointed out the British Army's progress through North Africa and every time there was a victory we moved the Army lines forward. Up until that time the Army had been going through a rough time and Rommel, the German Commander, had kept us 'on the run'. After several offensives matters began to improve and our brave Armies moved westward across North Africa.

Eileen and I attended a new school in Bath. It was actually a College - the Bath Technical College. The Admiralty had taken over our large College Building in the Centre of Bath and the school was operated in several Church Halls dotted all over the City. Sometimes we had to walk half a mile from one building to another for a different lesson.

We were amazed at life in Bath - so different from Gosport. It was like being in another world. For one thing, from 1942 onwards we experienced no more Air Raids and it seemed so peaceful after three years of hell in the south. In all fairness, I must state the Bathonians experienced a serious air raid, but that was before we moved there. There were very few air raid shelters. In addition, the shops were quite full of attractive goods. Cake shops had displays of cakes. My mother thought they were artificial (as in Gosport) but was told they were real, and what is more, were for sale! Needless to say we had plenty of cakes from then on, also tasted the delicious Bath Buns (yum! yum!) and the mineral water water biscuits. Oh! I forgot to mention that the Hot Springs which were used by the Romans for bathing are still in use. There are several swimming baths and the water at the time I was living there was delightfully warm for swimming, in addition the minerals in the water are very good for rheumatic troubles and stiff joints and aching muscles are relieved by bathing in these waters. There used to be a hospital in the centre of Bath called 'The Mineral Water Hospital' and patients from all over the country visited this hospital for treatment. There were several springs and this hospital was built over one of the springs. Sometimes steam could be seen rising from the ground indicating a hot spring nearby.

To help supplement our meals, Mum often purchased meat pies from the Cafeteria at the LMS Railway Station (London Midland and Scottish) and these pies could be bought without giving up 'points'. Mum was always shopping at the attractive shopping centre in Bath and looking out for items of food in an effort to give us a varied diet.

Unlike the city of Portsmouth there were no sailors in Bath. Of course there were many Naval Officers who were working very hard at the buildings requisitioned by the Admiralty. By this time, and following the bombing of Pearl Harbour there were many US Servicemen in England, and in Bath in particular there were literally thousands of US Army personnel in the City. They were everywhere; lots of them chewing gum and they appeared to earn a lot more money than our soldiers did. They seemed very nice and we were grateful to them for their efforts to assist us in freeing Europe. One presumes they were stationed outside the city and were training for the forthcoming landings in France.

The war news from South East Asia was very disturbing and about this time Manila in the Philippine Islands was taken by the Japanese, also New Guinea and the Solomon Islands. Singapore and Java surrendered to the Japanese and the position was very grave.

Dad bought some more maps of the Far East and also one of the World, and we marked on the map Russia's progress.

I have not mentioned Russia much. Hitler's Army invaded Russia and almost captured Moscow. Hitler required the oil fields in the Caucasus and the wheat of the Ukraine. The USSR was not prepared for war with Germany and retreated to Stalingrad. There was great suffering for every one in the occupied parts. At Stalingrad the Russians were able to stop the victorious German armies and gradually re-conquered the country. On 23 August 1943 Kharkov was re-captured, and when any town was captured the guns of Moscow fired as a sign of rejoicing. The King presented the people of Stalingrad with a Sword in recognition of the courageous way they faced the enemy.

Russia at this time was anxious for a second front to be started so that the heavy fighting which the country suffered would be relieved. Our main army was in North Africa and we were not at the time ready to invade France, but it was assumed that when we did the troops would cross the English Channel and land in the Calais area.

At school I made several very good friends and I was beginning to acquire a Somerset accent which caused amusement to my friends when I returned to Gosport. At school we had a very pleasant English teacher who suggested that instead of giving us English homework a couple of times a week, we should be allowed a whole term free from homework to enable us to write a book. We all voted that the book should be about Russia, our gallant ally. At the time I knew very little about this vast country so I spent many hours in the library at Bath researching the subject. The library overlooks the lovely river Avon, Weir and Pulteney

Bridge. From the maps Dad bought I was able to copy the outline of the coast of Russia and I made a big pull-out map.

The news on the radio was now a little different, at times our bombers and those of the US were bombing Germany, especially the Ruhr the very busy industrialised area of Germany - a different story. We felt the boot was on the other foot. One song emerged from this period, it was called *Lily Marlene*, a German song said to be a favourite with the German Army and now a favourite with our Army and the English people.

As time passed the whole of North Africa on the map on our wall was liberated and our 1st and 8th Armies were victorious. I could see on the map that the toe of Italy was not far from Tunisia and guessed we would land our invading army in the south of Italy. In fact on the 10th July 1943 the allies landed in Sicily, and soon after the Fascist Party in Italy was dissolved and by the 17th July Sicily was in Allied hands. A little while later the mainland was invaded and on 7th September Italy surrendered. However, fighting ensued for many months before we were able to capture Rome in June of 1944.

The five cinemas in Bath were always full both with civilians and US Servicemen who needed to relax, and the cinema was a very popular way to spend an evening or afternoon. The films seemed to be very good at the time. This was, of course before television was popular in the home. During the intervals the well known sound of the Glen Miller Band records could be heard and the lovely Moonlight Serenade was a great favourite and Bath was very much Americanised. Drinks were very short and it was impossible to buy whiskey. One day two Yanks had a bottle of whiskey and they were 'the worse for drink' and one of them dropped his bottle. This caused great annoyance to the residents who had forgotten what the spirit tasted like and they stood around the broken bottle to smell the aroma.

There were some items which it was impossible to purchase. A comb could not be found anywhere and the one remaining comb in our house was held by my father. Luckily, Mum Eileen and I were able to purchase a Dog's comb each. It was a great big thing made of some sort of metal and the teeth of the comb were quite wide apart. These combs lasted us for many years after the war ended.

In addition, it was impossible to purchase a rubber swimming cap and tennis balls were unobtainable. Eileen and I had a junior tennis racket each and we tried to roll a piece of old rubber into the shape of a ball and tied it with string. We then played with this object a kind of tennis in a park near our home. When we moved from Gosport to Bath we were keen members of the Girl Guides, but we did not rejoin the Guides in Bath. However, we were equally keen members of the St. John Ambulance Brigade and we did continue with our membership in Bath. We had already learned basic first aid and home nursing. Our uniforms were quite smart; grey dresses, black beret, white gloves, black shoes. On many Sundays we marched to Church in our uniforms on Church Parade with the rest of the youth of Bath. One day, following a parade we stood to attention in the courtyard of the Abbey and a smart lady in St. John Ambulance Uniform inspected us. She was about forty and she stopped to speak to me. Her name? Lady Louis Mountbatten, later known as Countess Mountbatten of Burma.

I forgot to mention earlier but the school meals service commenced early in the war and children could obtain their cooked lunches at school. When I was about fourteen I remember that most of the girls in my class took advantage of these school meals, but as I lived near the school I usually cycled home for my lunch. I sat down to my meal, had another look at the maps on the wall and my parents turned on the radio for the 1 pm news. The date was 6th JUNE 1944, and yes, you have guessed it, the Newsreader gave out on the radio details of the 'D Day' Landings by the Allies in France. All allied forces had combined to make this invasion possible. The armies had landed in the Cherbourg area in Normandy. I returned to school and told all my school chums the news and we realised that the light at the end of the tunnel could be seen and the war would soon draw to a close. It was an exciting time to think that our gallant forces and also those of the US and Dominions were liberating Europe,

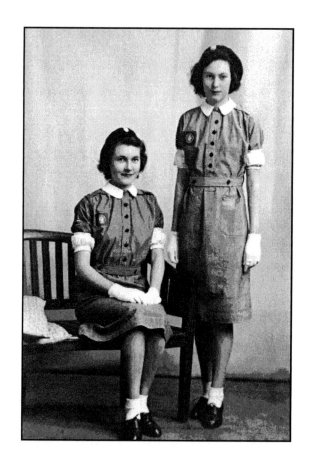

1943 - Bath
St. John's Ambulance Brigade

so long occupied by German forces. Needless to say we watched the Allies' progress on the map.

We sometimes returned to Gosport to make sure our house *Aurora* was OK and we also visited our relations. Sadly my old grandfather who had endured the terrible bombing died. The air raids had stopped and just prior to 6th June known as D Day, all the Forces gathered in the Gosport area ready for their departure to France. Our well known Beaches at Stokes Bay and another departure spot at Hardway were reinforced for all the heavy traffic. I was not in the area at the time but there are many stories about the army lorries which blocked the roads for days on end.

During the war, as a little girl, I had not met any Servicemen from the Commonwealth countries, but later when I visited Canberra in Australia and also New Zealand I was appalled to learn of the dreadful loss of life when young men in two world wars sacrificed their lives and rushed to our country's aid at our time of need. We will always owe them an extreme debt of gratitude.

Soon after the D Day Landings we moved from the rented house to a flat in the centre of Bath. It was in Nelson House right near the Parade Gardens, and we could often hear the music from our windows of the Service Bands which played in the Gardens by the River on Summer Afternoons. The exorbitant rent we paid was necessary as we could find no other accommodation. However, we did enjoy living in this luxury flat. Lord Horatio Nelson stayed in the house during a visit to Bath and there was a picture of Lady Hamilton on one of the walls. Eileen and I enjoyed window shopping during the summer evenings and the main shopping centre was a short walk from our home. We were still required to wear school uniform and clothing coupons were in short supply, as despite the fact that my parents appeared to have plenty of money I was unable to have lots of new clothes.

Round about this time Eileen left school and obtained a position at a well known High Street bank, or should I say Milsom Street Bank (the main road in Bath).

I continued with my school and we continued to walk from one building to another for different lessons. On one occasion a small group of us were walking near the shops and we noticed a long queue outside a sweet and tobacconist shop and found that Ice-creams were being sold. We none of us had tasted an ice-cream since 1939, so we forgot our classes and stood in the queue for about an hour-and-a-half and eventually managed to buy an ice-cream. It was delicious. One does not realize how much these little luxuries are missed. On return to school we explained to our English teacher the reason why we missed a lesson, and expected to be told off, instead the teacher said, alright girls you did the right thing, it is much more important for you to taste an ice-cream and it does not matter about missing a lesson. A very understanding teacher!

My father was still working hard at the Admiralty and several of his fellow Naval Officers lived in 'digs' away from their homes, and at times they felt lonely away from their families.

Mum was always trying to find a few tasty items in the shops and on occasions was able to buy some drinks, sherry etc. Our Naval Officer friends were often invited to Nelson House for parties and they very much enjoyed these gatherings. Because of my connections with the Navy, I decided that if the war continued and I was old enough I would like to join the W.R.N.S., especially as the young women in uniform used to look so smart.

It was beginning to look as though my wish to be a WREN in Wartime England would not be fulfilled. Still at school, our victorious Army, who had to fight so hard, liberated Paris on August 25th. Despite this the German Army was very strong and it seemed that the war would last forever. Shortly after this the first V2s fell on England. There was considerable damage in London by this new type of bomb.

At this time the school leaving age was 14 but my school course had not finished and I stayed at school until I was nearly sixteen, endeavouring me to acquire a sound commercial education.

During the first few months of 1945 the position in South East Asia looked very different, and the 'might of the sleeping giant' had certainly been aroused. The American forces re-captured many of the Islands which had been overrun by the Japanese.

In April we learned that Mussolini, the fascist ruler of Italy, had been shot by Italian partisans, and also a little later on the news broke that Hitler and his mistress had killed themselves.

Still at school I was glad to celebrate Victory on the 8th May 1945 known as VE Day (Victory in Europe Day). I could not possibly imagine life without a war. I had grown up in wartime England from the age of nine to fifteen, perhaps the most crucial years in a young girl's life.

Needless to say VE Day brought great rejoicing. In London thousands gathered in front of Buckingham Palace and soon the King and Queen and Princesses Elizabeth and Margaret appeared and received a mighty ovation. Then a familiar figure stood on the balcony between the King and Queen - Winston Churchill.

In a broadcast by the King on the Radio His Majesty said 'we give thanks to Almighty God for a great deliverance, speaking from our Empire's oldest capital city, war battered, but never for one moment daunted or dismayed - speaking from London I ask you to join with me in that act of thanksgiving. Germany the enemy who drove all Europe into war had been finally overcome. In the Far East we have yet to deal with the Japanese, a determined and cruel foe. To this we shall turn with the utmost resolve and with all our resources. But at this hour, when the dreadful shadow of war has passed from our hearths and homes in these Islands, we may at last make one pause for thanksgiving, and then turn our thoughts to the tasks all over the world which peace in Europe brings with it.'

His Majesty later said 'There is great comfort in the thought that the years of darkness and danger in which THE CHILDREN OF OUR COUNTRY HAVE GROWN UP are over please God FOR EVER.'

It was wonderful to be able to switch the lights on without blackout and we all found some Red White and Blue items and went into the street to celebrate with singing, dancing and street parties.

As the next few weeks passed by, details and pictures were released, also News Items on Cinema Screens, of the terrible atrocities in the Concentration Camps. It was a question of discussion whether young people should be allowed to see these pictures which were terrible. My teacher thought that we should make a point of seeing these films and never forget during the rest of our lives the terrible atrocities which had taken place.

As the summer holidays approached my school had arranged for a small group of girls to attend a harvest camp. This was a popular and cheap holiday and was designed to help the farming community. The school arranged for us to stay in a large barn and we were to work at neighbouring farms, and be paid for our work. This payment would go towards our food.

About the time the harvest camp arrangements

were made the news came that the first atomic bomb had fallen on Japan, and Hiroshima had been obliterated. A few days later another bomb dropped on Nagasaki. At this time Russia declared War on Japan and the whole might of the Allies was given to defeating Japan.

About the 11th August my school chums and I, accompanied by some teachers, caught the train from Bath Station to Devizes and proceeded to our 'Harvest Camp': I took my bicycle with me. We had the weekend to get settled and in an adjoining barn there were several Italian prisoners of war and they used the Barn for sleeping. They also worked on the land and we could often hear them singing Italian Songs. On the Monday a couple of us girls cycled to a nearby farm and soon started working on the harvest stooking. The next day we continued and I remember looking over the lovely Wiltshire countryside and thinking how peaceful England seemed and so lovely. Then the Church Bells started ringing and the whole valley sounded with the joyous sound. The reason? Japan had surrendered unconditionally to the Allies. The following day was a holiday. I had only worked one day and the Japanese surrendered. It was VJ Day.

I hope you have found my story of some interest. It is a long story, but, then it was a long war. I have heard terrible stories of people's experiences some in the desert during terrible sandstorms - others having to literally swim for their lives following the loss of their ships. The terrible fighting in the jungles of Burma. But I can't write about these experiences, only my own impressions of life during a World War for a little girl.

In the words of His Majesty King George VI on VE Day

PLEASE GOD OVER FOR EVER.

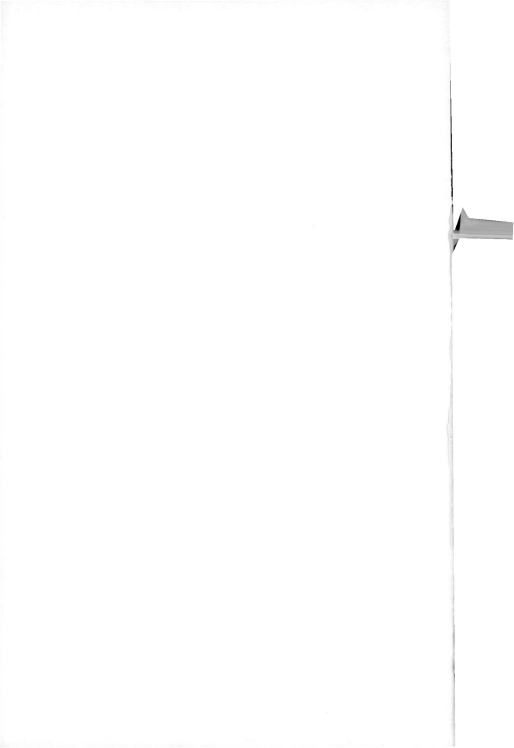